To Josy

CW01391343

Late Shift at the Pickle Factory

Hope you enjoy
Love Mary x

Mary Dickins

Burning Eye

BurningEyeBooks
Never Knowingly
Mainstream

This edition published by Burning Eye Books 2023

www.burningeye.co.uk

@burningeyebooks

Burning Eye Books
15 West Hill, Portishead, BS20 6LG

ISBN 978-1-913958-38-1

Printed and bound by CPI Group (UK) Ltd, Croydon, CR0 4YY

Late Shift at the Pickle Factory

Contents

Prayer   9
Easy Street   10
What Dolly Taught Me   11
On Finding an Unused Melon Scoop   12
Attention, All Passengers   13
Eulogy for an Idol (Mashup)   14
Beds   15
Late Shift at the Pickle Factory   16
Spice   17
Portrait of Her Boyfriend as a Barnacle   18
Childhood   19
Cake Hole   20
A Map of Me   21
Bomb Scare   22
Unintentional Sonnet   23
Things I Would Rather Do Than
    Try and Write a Sonnet   24
The Chambermaid's Lament   25
Pam Has a Bad Day   26
Hoover Care Instructions   27
EasyJet Speedy Boarders   28
Haikus for a Sick Friend   29
Time for a Riddle   30
Seeing Red   31
He Forgot the Parmesan   32
Singing the Messiah   33
Curmudgeon   34
Health Check   35
Vox Pop Snow   36
Bearbnb   37
Praise Poem   38
Interrogating the Poem   39
Shit Creek   40

Prayer

Dear Tech Gods
who art in cyberspace,
hallowed be thy fibres.
Thy 5G come;
thy will be done on Zoom as it is on WhatsApp.
Give us this day our daily connection
and forgive us our data protection
as we forgive broadband providers who trespass against us,
and lead us not into tech fail but deliver us from malfunctions,
for thine is the bandwidth, the algorithm and the server.
Amen.

Easy Street

on easy street we bend the rules
while basking in infinity pools – on easy street
we blame the poor and insecure
our wealth is safely stashed offshore – on easy street
so many homes we hire jets
to ferry round our pampered pets – on easy street
we wheel and deal and hedge our bets
and build a few more buy-to-lets – on easy street
and all the while we suffer fools
because they went to public schools – on easy street
and we complain that life is hard
while slurping oysters at the Shard – on easy street
without a care we only cry
when bonuses are not so high – on easy street
for we believe that our net worth
is not an accident of birth – on easy street
we disregard that silver spoon
inserted whilst inside the womb – on easy street
we feast on culinary foam
and thank our swanky chromosomes – on easy street
we have to steal your pension pot
to keep the housing market hot – on easy street
we raise the bar and call the tune
ensuring our eternal boom – on easy street

What Dolly Taught Me

Dolly showed me how to face the storm and look for rainbows.
That people see boobs, not brains, but two can play that game.
She told me never to be a rung on someone else's ladder.
She taught me big hair and giveaway smiles,
when to keep your man and when to run.
Not to harden my heart but to strengthen the muscles around it.
She told me to find my style and stick to it forever,
that there is never a time not to love.
She sent me a pillow to dream on and filled it with courage.

I haven't always done what Dolly says,
even though she can pluck me like a twelve-string.
I settled for rhinestones when there were diamonds to be had.
I never could dance in heels and I can't reach the high notes,
but today I am cruising east London in the back of an Uber,
singing 'Jolene' along with the driver, and everything
is all right with the world despite the endless rain.

On Finding an Unused Melon Scoop

She'd dreamt of being more refined,
held dinner parties in her mind.
A fine repast her guests
would clap whilst slugging
Châteauneuf-du-Pape.
A melon entrée was her plan,
mozzarella, Parma ham,
some lightly simmered langoustines,
a tarte Tatin with brandy cream.
She'd glow with pride whilst loading plates
and handing round the After Eights.
In truth her life was far less glam,
her aspirations purely sham.
The table hardly ever laid.
No fragrant moules or marinades.
She never baked a Dover sole
or served a Scottish salmon whole
or stirred an ossobuco slick
with meaty gravy rich and thick.
Ham, egg and chips, fish finger baps
and pesto pasta perched on laps.
No culinary heights were scaled.
Potential guests remained unmailed.
Yet in her kitchen drawer still sits
this smug, reproachful bit of kit.
It saddens her that overall
in her whole life there's been no call
for deftly sculpted melon balls
and now the cost of living's fucked
there might not even be enough
to eat tonight.

Attention, All Passengers

Attention, all passengers: please do not leave
your emotional baggage unattended.
We are pleased to announce that there is on-board
entertainment on all our trains – it's called a window.
We are pleased to announce that there is on-board
entertainment on all our trains – it's called other passengers.
Passengers are advised to mind the gap
between the timetable and reality.
We would like to remind passengers that crying
on the concourse is discouraged as it makes it slippery.
Whilst we apologise for the delay, we would like to remind
passengers that time is a mystifying and fluid concept.
This is a health and safety announcement:
nothing is safe. I repeat: nothing is safe.
The 7.15 has been delayed due to leaves on the line;
they fluttered in fragile freefall, their vivid hues
of brown and red carpeting the tracks in glory.
Passengers are reminded that manspreading is not permitted
and may result in your being asked to leave the train.
The first-class accommodation available on this train
is clearly identifiable by the headrests – that's the only difference.
We regret to announce that due to essential maintenance work
the driver of the 8.55 has been delayed.
On behalf of all staff and passengers, we would like to remind you
of our common humanity.
Please ensure that you leave all your valuables on the train.
We will collect them later.

Eulogy for an Idol (Mashup)

She was a fat girl, always being picked on by the other girls at school, but she sang as if her heart were damaged beyond repair. Many tortuous conclusions resulted. For example, she decided that there seemed to be no future in the status quo and predicted worldwide rioting in the street and the meltdown of nuclear reactors. Once this manifesto was completed it was never again altered. All events and developments were made to fit her worldview. Soon she was relegated to a black hole from which no cultural light escaped.

A remarkable transformation took place when a pulp paperback revealed the true extent of her scorn and indifference. She had lost several stone and acquired armfuls of tattoos when, defying expectations almost as a kind of sport, she fused street-level urgency with elements of European avant-garde. Hammering out piano ostinato and using her viola to produce grating drones, her hymns to transgressive behaviour pushed her to beyond cult status. She lurched on as best she could – her talent unquenched.

Marrying beauty and noise, her idiosyncratic artistic impulses created an audience of outsiders who coalesced around her example. Her appeal transcended language barriers, and she made alienation the dominant mode and an article of faith for subsequent generations. Her final public appearance came three days before her death, when she danced in dreamy circles and disappeared without singing a note. Throughout her career she longed for a way out of that mask, wig and dress.

Beds

their first one was an unknown country eagerly explored
they slept as lovers do wrapped in each other's charms

their second one was a nest for small invaders
a playground and sometimes a trampoline

their third one was a battleground where they slept
back to fuming back tugging the stolen covers to and fro

their fourth one was bigger he said she slept like a starfish she
said he snored occasionally they still rubbed together for comfort

their fifth one was a sickbed they used various pillow formations
to stack arthritic limbs into better alignment

the sixth one was a vortex with an icy patch where once
there was warm body to wrap around

she never slept on his side in case by doing so she inadvertently
erased the shape he had made in this world

Late Shift at the Pickle Factory

Only foreigners will do it, says Murat,
leading me onto the cacophonous factory floor.
The air is dense with the stench of sauerkraut and vinegar.
You won't stay, says Murat. *They never do.*
He walks me to a shallow trough full of gherkins
bobbing like shoals of sea cucumbers
alongside a conveyor belt. A procession
of nearly full jars glide eagerly on their journey
to the capper where a piston clamps on the lids
with an emphatic mechanical sigh.
The last gherkin is problem, Murat says. *Customer wants full jar.*
Machine can't do. Gherkin in wrong place means kaput.
As he speaks a jar is crushed to smithereens.
No gloves, says Murat. *Make hands slippy.*
Everything stops as the broken glass is cleared.

The late shift. Eight hours punctured by a twenty-minute dash
to a canteen where even the chocolate tastes of pickle.
I struggle with the pace but soon I become an automaton,
placing each gherkin precisely and not protruding from the lip.
Vinegar slops from the side of the trough,
drenches my skimpy apron, soaks my shoes.
My hands are wrinkled and pale from prolonged dousing,
my fingernails soft and bleached.
A noxious smell takes up residence
in my nostrils despite ample showering.
At the hostel someone complains that I
have made the washing machine smell of vinegar.
My dreams are invaded by giant gherkins.
My pores leak vinegar instead of sweat.
Saturday morning and I queue outside the dingy agency.
A pittance is delivered in a plain brown envelope.
As I count it I notice that a fingernail has begun to peel off.
I don't go back. Murat was right, and every time I see a gherkin
floating in that gruesome essence   I remember him.

Spice

Even though we were English now,
there was huge excitement whenever
the cardboard boxes marked *fragile* arrived from India.
Inside, cradled in tissue paper,
nestled fiery pepper balls, green cardamoms,
their skin redolent with resin, earthy cumin seeds,
dried chillies and bags of yellow turmeric
as vivid as powdered sunshine.
Even though we were English now,
my family would fall upon the boxes
like starving animals.
Even though we were English now,
in the days that followed the kitchen would be filled
with steam and the tantalising aromas
of mulligatawny soup and fragrant biryanis.
Even though we were English now,
as we feasted the conversation would be enlivened
by jovial and affectionate tales of Ooty, Yercaud, Bangalore
and of people whose names had become familiar to me
only as ghosts that shared our lives.
Even though we were English now,
as the spices diminished so did our contentment, and
as inevitable as indigestion would come
the aftermath of tension and poorly disguised grief.
Even though she was English now, my mother's tears
could peel the wallpaper off the concrete walls of our prefab.
Even though he was English now,
I would watch my father trudge down the path to work
as though he carried a whole country on his back.
I was born under these grey, wretched skies.
My only soundtrack was the din of the Old Kent Road.
At school I ate minced beef and bland semolina.
I could never comprehend exactly who or what had been lost.

Portrait of Her Boyfriend as a Barnacle

she was a wreck when he found her
thrust by bitter winds she had floundered
only to be grounded by the moonstruck tide
rudderless and stranded her precious hulk
listing dangerously from foremast to mizzen
her splintered keel entrenched in the silted ocean floor
ragged sails flapping useless in the breeze
her cargo long since plundered

then came this curious crustacean
who made hard and fast to her hull who
resisted her disdainful and repeated attempts
to prise his stubborn exoskeleton from her bows
who insisted that she would come to cherish
the contours of his crenulated carapace
his graceful filtering filaments
the rare delicacy of his inner flesh
and the secretion of his sticky phosphoproteins
without which she would certainly disintegrate

now they are elemental lovers fused fast
even as lightning storms flicker around them
and they are slowly trashed by the ocean swell
and for his splendid and enduring perseverance
she remains eternally grateful

Childhood

my playground was a bomb crater
my teacher was a monk
my family were aliens
my friends were urchins
my teddy bear was threadbare
my socks fell down
my key let me in after school
my fingers were frozen
my dinner came out of tins
I had a cheeky grin

Cake Hole

supposing there is a little girl who is trudging home from school when she comes across a cardboard box in the middle of the empty street and she prises open the lid and sees it brim-full of sachets of instant vanilla sponge mix and because this is by far the best thing that has happened to her for a long while she disregards its questionable origin and clutching it to her chest she scuttles home and stows it in the furthest corner of the larder where her father never looks and in those lonely hours after school rather than waiting listlessly for his keys to rattle in the lock or huddling in the library until it closes or following other children home and pretending she lives with them instead she tears open a packet adds an egg and bakes and eats a whole cake that nobody knows about but her and sometimes she smothers it with jam or golden syrup or cling peaches or sprinkles it with a delicate snow of coconut flakes but mostly she crams it whole and unadorned into her rapacious mouth and thus she comes to crave this daily ritual and the sweet anticipatory haze that wafts its way through the warm kitchen followed by the cloying comfort of cake in her belly but then what if midway through her treasure trove she catches herself gorging ecstatically in the mirror and from then on she is troubled by her gluttony and the pallid yellow of the mixture and the sickly sight and smell of it make her heave and the flabbiness of the sponge so disgusts her that she discards the remainder of her loot squashing it furtively into the dustbin and what if she draws a line under this interlude and she does not even recall it until many years later when a random nudge thrusts it bobbing to the surface and in that moment she reflects that she should have learnt an important lesson in life from this episode because although she had quickly come to realise that you cannot fill a gaping mother-shaped hole with cake this has never stopped her repeating the same pitiful and pointless experiment with an extensive range of other dubious and ill-advised substances

A Map of Me

I wish I was Barcelona, all style and swagger
and gigantic gothic towers that siphon your breath away,
all flamenco tapping and frantic guitar strumming and
cosmopolitan chatter and rustic bread and tomatoes
drizzled with silky oil and history crammed into every corner,
held aloft by flamboyance and bravado, multihued and unashamed.

I like to think I'm Liverpool, a tad debilitated and run-down
but so friendly, all come in and have a brew. I'm a bit of a scally,
all art deco palace and back-to-back houses
and people chanting you'll never walk alone in pubs and terraces.
I'm slip you a tenner if you're short and deadpan humour
and pride making light of unease and desperation.

Secretly I'm Dungeness,
all leave me alone while I stare broodily into the bleak horizon,
all wind gusting across salty shingle
and the sun going down by the nuclear power station
and marsh harriers, whooper swans and gulls
swooping over the temperamental brine.

I'm sea kale and wood sage pushing through
as the grey frothy tide recedes into the distance.

Bomb Scare

on the post-natal ward we all lie bleeding our babies swaddled in bassinets beside each bed and I find myself watching the mother opposite because she hasn't changed and the back of her nightdress is blood-streaked and she seems bewildered and her baby is pallid and fretful and refusing the breast but then we are summoned wincing and waddling to the breakfast table where having little else in common the talk is of stitches and competing ordeals until the conversation turns to the names we are choosing and when we look to the bewildered woman for an answer she hesitates and then she says *I'm calling her Enola Gay[1] I love that song* and the others say *that's nice* and then they *ooh* and *aah* and somebody ta-das the tune and a shiver runs through me because I am thinking of a monstrous fireball reducing bodies to burnt shadows on the pavements as a burgeoning cloud sheds uranium across a helpless city and I am thinking of generations of babies just like ours dying slowly as radiation sickness seeps into every living cell but on reading the room there is not a flicker of recognition so *that's lovely* I say belatedly because why should I be the one to tell her although surely someone must and also because to do so at this moment would be to drop another kind of bomb into the proceedings however to this day my guilt persists and sometimes just to make myself feel better I picture little Enola Gay growing older and she is laughing and playing happily in the sunshine and I pray it is true but somehow I doubt it

---

1 Enola Gay was the name of the B-29 bomber that dropped the atomic bomb on Hiroshima and also the name of a 1980s hit single by Orchestral Manoeuvres in the Dark.

Unintentional Sonnet

this poem is the opposite of money
this poem is a cracked smile in sepia
this poem is a shock absorber
this poem sings an aria in the distance
this poem is a friend to the soft earth
this poem is a giddy drop into a plunge pool
this poem is lipstick smeared on the rims of glasses
this poem is a phone ringing in Budapest
this poem has clumsy sex with acquaintances
this poem is the past lapping at your shoulder

this poem makes you reach for a semicolon
this poem requires urgent clarification
this poem never intended to be a sonnet
this poem would like to offer you another appointment

Things I Would Rather Do Than Try and Write a Sonnet

for Jacqueline Saphra

I'd rather give a mad baboon a squeeze,
at Wembley sing a tuneless made-up song,
play bagatelle and only use my knees
or prod a senior policeman with a prong,
adopt Edwina Currie as a mate
or bunny-hop along the Pennine Way,
eat cat food from a filthy broken plate,
consume a toothsome spider's egg soufflé,
go jogging in my jersey dayglo tights
to places where I really don't belong;
perhaps a stroll across the Golan Heights?
I try so much and still I get it wrong.

Infernal form; I blame the bloody bard.
He made it look so easy, but it's hard.

The Chambermaid's Lament

Any resemblance to a famous show tune is purely intentional.

They asked me if I knew
how to clean a loo.
I described with pride
techniques I have tried,
fluids I've applied.

They said some days you'll find
pubic hairs entwined,
toenails on the floor,
semen stains galore.
Bleach gets in your eyes.

If management decide
to take me for a ride
I'll be out the door.
Rather be a whore.
Bleach gets in your eyes.

Pam Has a Bad Day

Man rang Pam, says am Sam.
Sam says bank says cash astray.
Sam, all charm, wants a grand.
Pah! says Pam. *What a prank!*
Pam's a savvy ma'am,
says, *Stay away, Sam, thanks.*

Man rang Pam, all drama,
says Jack, says PayPal.
Jack, smarmy, says app crash.
Jack wants Pam's data.
Fancy that! says canny Pam.
Bad karma crank calls!
Tacky task, Jacky!
Hasta la vista, baby, cracks Jack back.

Man rang Pam.
Pam ratty and hasty snarls – all sarcasm.
Wham bam scam? Want stash? Want data?
Damn tawdry twat!
What? says man
Pam, all barmy, calls man
crappy cad!
Skanky pants!
Swamp spawn!
Nasty mangy plank!

Calm, Pammy, says man, all aghast, frankly.
Am DAD.

Hoover Care Instructions

A found poem.

So you find yourself struggling on.
Give it a bit of love. The last thing
you want is the muck exploding
all over your newly spotless rug.
We've all been there, so let it cool down first.
Be gentle but firm, and if there's a line stick to it.
Look at the bottom and you'll be horrified
at the amount of bumph that gets stuck.
Trust me, you do not want to have to deal
with the consequences. Suck it up.
Pull the nastiness off more often.
That will be the path of least resistance.
Air has to pass through all the gunk.
Obviously dislodge any obstructions.

This advice also applies to relationships.

EasyJet Speedy Boarders

We're easyJet Speedy Boarders! Make way! Let us through!
We got ourselves an upgrade just to get in front of you.
It's us who had the foresight. It's us who had the dosh
to get ahead of the rabble, thereby avoiding the squash.

We're easyJet Speedy Boarders. Our tickets say SB!
We spent a few quid to feel better than you
because nothing in life is free.

It's us who get the window seat. It's us who see the Alps.
Everyone else can go to hell and loll in the aisle like tramps.
Because we're easyJet Speedy Boarders. We get all the breaks.
You get the seat near the toilet or the malfunctioning one that shakes.

We're easyJet Speedy Boarders. We're scrambling through the door.
We will compete to reach the seat our excess charge was for.
So long, all you suckers left by the boarding gate.
It's us who get to choose our seats. It's you who have to wait.

We're easyJet Speedy Boarders, high in the clouds once more.
We got the extra legroom and we're by the emergency door.

Haikus for a Sick Friend

stuck in the slow lane
all incapacitated
while courage gathers

time hangs so slow for
the reluctantly inert
in that tired space

too soon comes roaring
the fevered wellness of life
in the faster lane

so avoid traffic
get the highway rerouted
through your underpass

Time for a Riddle

How do you move?
I trickle like water.
What do you sound like?
The tread of a stranger on a dark stairwell.
What is your function?
The avoidance of collisions.
How do you rule?
By absolute dictatorship.
How shall I know you?
A tap on the shoulder – a cold handshake.
Shall we dance?
Tango or slow jive?
How should I hold you?
Like an egg in the palm of your hand.
What do you taste like?
Best savoured in tiny morsels.
When do you sleep?
Not when you do.
Can you be counted?
How long have you got?
When will you end?
I never miss a beat.

Seeing Red

the first time she saw red
she was a slow dancer
in a ravaged land
they called her visionary
and named her after their dreams

the second time she saw red
they slandered her a firebrand
who just happened to be caught
in a twisted arabesque
on the ruddy clay

the last time she saw red
her lacerated reflection
was strangled by a tangled rope
she wielded hoops on tiptoe then
tumbled gratefully into the abyss

the light that day was magnificent

He Forgot the Parmesan

first he painted the sky blue for her then
he tickled her favourite hen until it sang
he brought grape juice his feet still stained from the pressing
he made a summer pudding and placed it on the picnic
blanket
by the spaghetti sleek with olive oil and spiked with basil
he brought a photo of her parents waving farewell
and a rolling pin to scare away their ghosts

the band strummed and squeezed a sunset duet
all this while the camping kettle belched steam
he trembled as he led her to the woodland spot
you forgot the parmesan again she whined
and all the love in him began to shrivel
and the engagement ring in his back pocket
scorched a circle on his tender skin

Singing the Messiah

see this is what
you need to know about me
even though it has never been told
I've been strangled from birth
so sometimes my voice sounds reedy
my flayed vocal cords so limp from screaming
hang loose as the strings of a clapped-out violin

but hell I'll sing with you
I'll gather in the square
the sky for rafters
I'll cloak myself in pallid wintry light
while those thunderous tones
applaud an absent god
and your rapturous voices soar
towards each euphoric crescendo

the high notes might hover beyond my reach
but even if my fractured voice should fail me
I'll be in the back row
wearing a beauteous face
mouthing hallelujahs

Curmudgeon

Irascible codger
Face like a gourd
Relishes a bad omen

Perpetual doommonger
Tendency to drone
Hates anything modern

Parsimonious and dour
Often begs to demur
Totally without decorum

Never willingly nude
Will be sorely missed

Health Check

Your veins are full of butter. Your body mostly lard.
Teeth like wire cutters. Arteries rock-hard.
Your body mostly lard. You've never heard of kale.
Arteries rock-hard. You've broken all the scales.

You've never heard of kale. Your breath is rank with smoke.
You've broken all the scales. Your diet is a joke.
Your breath is rank with smoke. You love a Milky Way.
Your diet is a joke. Ever heard of five a day?

You love a Milky Way. You say quinoa makes you gag.
Ever heard of five a day? You won't give up the fags.
You say quinoa makes you gag. You claim whisky keeps you sane.
You won't give up the fags or the Friday night cocaine.

It appears that what you fancy has set your spirit free.
So have another pasty. After all, you're ninety-three.

Vox Pop Snow

Day One
Isn't it beautiful?
Hope it settles.
Sooo quiet!
Where's that toboggan?
Send that photo to Countryfile.
The biggest snowman in the street!
Magic!

Day Two
Where's the grit?
Train cancelled!
Out of broccoli in Tesco.
Stuck on A30!
They manage in Canada, don't they?
Only a sprain.
Tragic!

Bearbnb

A cosy watertight den.
Sleeps one.
Available October to May.
Secluded location.
Nearest hive three hundred metres.
Please note:
no parties.
Guests are required to shit in the woods.

Praise Poem

In praise of every refugee on every boat that sank
and anyone that has to get their supper from a bank.

In praise of those who greet each morning challenged and impaired
and anyone who stands their ground to show they really care.

In praise of every worker insecure with little pay
and anyone on benefits who struggles through each day.

In praise of those without a roof camped out in our streets
and anyone who gives a damn and helps them to their feet.

In praise of those considered mad, the helpless and conflicted
and victims of immoral laws wrongfully convicted.

In praise of younger citizens who seldom get a say.
In praise of every elder made to feel they've had their day.

In praise of those in mouldy flats condemned to sit and shiver
and those who tread our weary streets with items to deliver.

In praise of the precarious squeezed by reckless greed
and anyone who's found themselves belittled for their needs.

We calibrate society in favour of the winners; please
endorse this accolade for those more sinned against than sinners.

Interrogating the Poem

Are you villanelle? Elegy?
Ballad or sonnet? Sestina? Triolet? Ode?
Blank verse or concrete? Pantoum or pastoral?
Any particular mode?
Ironic, Byronic, laconic or physical?
Satirical, emotive or profound?
Do you enhance a political stance?
Should I expand and expound?
Are you fickle, just a trickle?
Are you hurricane or breeze?
Obsessive and excessive?
Trying much too hard to please?
Are you frantic or pedantic?
Maudlin and mundane? Lacking passion?
Slave to fashion? Naive or urbane?
Do you scan? Should you rhyme?
Do you have clear parameters?
Should I have maintained that iambic pentameter?
Are your concepts entwined? Are your metaphors mined?
Will your references chime with enough humankind?
Are your sources diverse? Are those adverbs a curse?
Are you doomed to rejigging until you are worse?
Should I tear you to pieces? Retract and rewind?
Can you pull yourself together? Is it time?

Did they clap?

Were they just being kind?

Shit Creek

when I am hollow from disaster
steeped in tragedy
limp from the treacherous stench of betrayal
swaying by the river of unreason

when the depths of my love exhaust me

I weave my canoe from silver linings
stripped from thunderous black cloud
I paddle up shit creek to happiness
staying one step ahead of the flood

Notes

'Eulogy for an Idol' was first published in the anthology *Inspirational Idols*, edited by Donna Samworth (Forward Poetry, 2016).

'Seeing Red' was first published online by Visual Verse: https://visualverse.org/submissions/seeing-red/

'He forgot the Parmesan' was first published online by Visual Verse: https://visualverse.org/submissions/i-forgot-the-parmesan/

'Health Check' was first published online by Spilling Cocoa over Martin Amis: https://www.spillingcocoa.com/health-check-by-mary-dickins/

Acknowledgements

Thanks to my talented daughter for an amazing cover; to my poetry friends for their support and encouragement; to Bridget Hart and Clive Birnie for believing in me; to Mo, Hannah and Theo for all the love you give, and to anyone reading my words.